45 Affordable Retirement Towns

Best U.S. Towns for Retirement on a Budget

Written and Edited by Kris Kelley

D0665381

To My Mother

Published by

Webwerxx, Inc.

17101 E. Baltic Dr., Aurora, Colorado 80013

Copyright © 2015-2016 by Webwerxx, Inc.

All rights reserved. No part of this publication may be reproduced in any way without the express written consent of Webwerxx, Inc.

Notice

This publication contains information from numerous sources. Every effort has been made to verify the accuracy of the information in this book, but some information, particularly median home prices and cost of living numbers, may have changed since publication. As a result, Webwerxx, Inc. cannot guarantee the accuracy of the content contained within this publication.

ISBN-13: 978-1505524437

Cover Image: © tasia12/123RF.COM

Table of Contents

Introduction

Great places to retire are located throughout the United States, but many of these places are expensive and out of reach for the average American. In the wake of the Great Recession, retirees are seeking affordable towns where their budget will stretch further. A less expensive town, however, has to have more than just low or average living costs.

Any town considered as a retirement destination should also have well-tended neighborhoods, recreational and/or cultural amenities, a local or nearby public library, a low or average crime rate, local or nearby accredited medical facilities and a welcoming quality that makes it a desirable place to live. Here we have 45 towns that meet these criteria. No one town is perfect, however, so we also take a look at each town's drawbacks.

Generally speaking, the South and the Midwest are the most affordable regions of the United States. Most of the towns included in this book are in these regions, and most of the towns are in states that are considered tax-friendly for retirement. The few towns that are in less tax-friendly states may have living costs low enough to offset the higher taxes.

Alabama

Centre, Alabama

Deep in the backwoods of Cherokee County in northeastern Alabama, the air is thick and damp, and the fragrance of magnolias and honeysuckle is unmistakable. Here, not far from the Georgia border, life unfolds slowly in sleepy Centre.

Nearby Weiss Lake, 33,000 acres of clean, blue water, is known as "The Crappie Capitol of The World," and it is the area's lifeblood. It is the reason people who were born here stay here and the reason why newcomers relish this unhurried spot far off the beaten path.

Residents are practical and down to earth, and crime is not much of a concern. High school football games, barbeque outings and fish cookouts are popular. The downtown sits along wide Main Street, which is lined by one and two story red brick buildings that house city offices, retailers and banks.

Several festivals take place every year, including the Fall Festival in October and the Taste of Cherokee in February. The Cherokee County Historical Museum chronicles the County's heritage and has a Starbucks and an internet cafe.

Restaurants are mostly fast food places and home-style diners, but Tony's Steak Barn serves slabs of steak and receives rave reviews. Shopping is limited to a few large grocery markets, Walgreens, Walmart and the like.

Population: 3,500 (city proper)

Percentage of Population Age 45 or Better: 50%

Cost of Living: 10% below the national average

Median Home Price: $115,000

Climate: Summer temperatures reach into the 90s, and winter temperatures are in the 30s, 40s and 50s. On average, the area receives 58 inches of rain per year.

At Least One Hospital Accepts Medicare Patients? Yes

At Least One Hospital Accredited by Joint Commission? Yes

Public Transit: No

Crime Rate: Below the national average

Public Library: Yes

Political Leanings: Conservative

Is Alabama Considered Tax Friendly for Retirement? Yes

Cons: Alabama is a poor state, and Centre's poverty rate is above the national average. The chance of a tornado striking is 235% higher than the national average.

Notes: Centre is a good spot if searching for an unhurried pace with plenty of fishing.

Arizona

Casas Adobes, Arizona

This unincorporated community is one of Tucson's oldest areas, and it is distinctly suburban. It sits just to the east of Interstate 10 and has mountains to its east and west.

Developed in the 1940s by Sam Nanini, the town is primarily known for Nanini's Casas Adobes Plaza. This upscale dining and retail hub attracts visitors from around the region.

Tohono Chul Park, a botanic garden in the heart of Casas Adobes, links nature and art through its exhibits and has daily tours, birding walks, Xeriscape lessons and a seasonal concert series. The nearby Catalina State Park, sprinkled with saguaros, is a sanctuary for desert wildlife. It boasts an equestrian center, canyons, streams, camping sites and miles of trails.

Numerous golf courses, including the Lee Trevino-designed Crooked Tree Golf Course, dot the community. Another dozen golf courses are in the surrounding area.

Residential architectural styles include adobe, Southwestern and Mediterranean. Most of Casas Adobes' homes have Xeriscaping.

Population: 69,000 (city proper)

Percentage of Population Age 45 or Better: 40%

Cost of Living: 1% below the national average

Median Home Price: $175,000

Climate: Summer temperatures reach the low-100s, and winter temperatures are in the 30s, 40s and 50s. On average, the area receives 11 inches of rain per year.

At Least One Hospital Accepts Medicare Patients? No, but Tucson has several hospitals that accept Medicare patients.

At Least One Hospital Accredited by Joint Commission? No, but Tucson has several hospitals that are accredited.

Public Transit: No

Crime Rate: Meets the national average

Public Library: Yes

Political Leanings: Liberal

Is Arizona Considered Tax Friendly for Retirement? Yes

Cons: None

Notes: Some people say that Casas Adobes does not have much of an identity. Westward Look Grand Resort and Spa overlooks Casas Adobes from the Santa Catalina foothills.

Clarkdale, Arizona

Both the Verde River and Bitter Creek flow through central Arizona's historic Clarkdale. This high country hamlet was built as a company town in 1912 to house a smelter and the workers for the Clark family copper mine and survives primarily because of its surrounding natural beauty.

Located near the Tuzigoot National Monument and the Sycamore Canyon Wilderness, which is home to ring-tailed cats, black bears and scorpions, Clarkdale affords plenty of opportunities for hiking, biking and backcountry camping. Verde Canyon has 80 fishable miles and is popular with kayakers. The Verde Canyon Railroad also makes excursions through parts of the canyon.

Clarkdale's downtown is small but has shops and restaurants. The town hosts free concerts every summer, and the Verde Valley Theatre has a full season of comedy and drama. Made in Clarkdale is an organization that hosts one of Arizona's finest annual art shows.

Neighborhoods are somewhat ill defined, but historic homes and modest ranch ramblers are common in town. On the edges of town, planned neighborhoods with attractive adobe-style, Mediterranean-style and Southwestern-style homes are the norm.

Yavapai College has an Osher Life Learning Institute (OLLI), and it offers a variety of peer-directed classes for all ages, including retirees. During baseball season, the parks and recreation department offers bus rides to Arizona Diamondback games in Phoenix.

Population: 4,100 (city proper)

Percentage of Population Age 45 or Better: 27%

Cost of Living: Meets the national average

Median Home Price: $180,000

Climate: Summer temperatures are in the 90s and low-100s, and winter temperatures are in the 30s, 40s and 50s. On average, Clarkdale receives 12 inches of rain and 4 inches of snow per year. The elevation is 3,545 feet above sea level.

At Least One Hospital Accepts Medicare Patients? No, but Verde Valley Medical Center is 5 miles away in Cottonwood and accepts Medicare patients.

At Least One Hospital Accredited by Joint Commission? No, but Verde Valley Medical Center is 5 miles away in Cottonwood and is accredited by DNV Healthcare.

Public Transit: Yes, provided by CAT

Crime Rate: Below the national average

Public Library: Yes

Political Leanings: Conservative

Is Arizona Considered Tax Friendly for Retirement? Yes

Cons: None

Notes: Most shopping and services are found in Cottonwood, about 5 miles away.

Glendale, Arizona

Homesteaders first came to the desert land that is now Glendale in 1882 and built a canal. The new community attracted Russian, Mexican and Japanese farmers, but it was not until the 1940s when Luke Field (now Luke Air Force Base) was built that Glendale began to grow.

These days Glendale is only 9 miles northwest of downtown Phoenix and still has a diverse population. It has all the amenities of a big city and is home to two pro-sports teams: the National Football League's Arizona Cardinals and the National Hockey League's Phoenix Coyotes.

Glendale also manages the MLB's spring training facility, Camelback Ranch. Both the Jobing.com arena and the University of Phoenix Stadium are state-of-the-art sport facilities and host everything from wrestling tournaments to lacrosse competitions.

The Catlin and Old Towne districts have large concentrations of antique shops, but there are also big box store centers and malls. Residents enjoy 7 public pools, a group of dog parks and 2 golf courses.

The city supports a symphony, a desert botanic garden and multiple performing groups. Glendale's Chocolate Affaire and Jazz and Blues Festival have national reputations.

Regional parks such as Thunderbird Mountain and Estrella Mountain have hiking trails and dramatic desert views. Several community colleges have a Glendale address.

Neighborhoods are varied, some very attractive and some less desirable. Generally, older sections of town have small ranch ramblers. Newer neighborhoods are on the north end of town and include Arrowhead Ranch, a master-planned community with Mediterranean-style homes.

Population: 227,000 (city proper)

Percentage of Population Age 45 or Better: 27%

Cost of Living: 1% below the national average

Median Home Price: $155,000

Climate: This area has very hot summers and mild winters. Summer temperatures are in the 90s and low-100s, and winter temperatures are in the 60s and 70s. On average, Glendale receives 9 inches of rain per year.

At Least One Hospital Accepts Medicare Patients? Yes

At Least One Hospital Accredited by Joint Commission? Yes

Public Transit: Yes, and its light-rail system has a planned opening date of 2026.

Crime Rate: Meets the national average

Public Library: Yes

Political Leanings: Conservative

Is Arizona Considered Tax Friendly for Retirement? Yes

Cons: The air quality is poor. Some people say that Glendale lacks a sense of identity.

Notes: Luke AFB is the only active duty F-16 training base in the world.

Yuma, Arizona

Yuma is in the very southwestern tip of Arizona and for many years was a busy ferry stop and crossing point on the Colorado River. In 1849 alone, up to 80,000 people passed through Yuma on their way to the California gold fields.

These days this desert city is primarily a tourist and "snowbird" destination and tends to come alive during the winter months. The downtown is attractive and has government buildings, a small museum, wineries, restaurants, pottery shops and cafes.

Shopping and dining options are plentiful, and the Yuma Art Center brings a bit of culture. The Paradise Casino has a bar, a restaurant and entertainment that often includes karaoke nights and boxing bouts.

The Colorado River Regatta, the Caballeros de Yuma Colorado River Crossing Festival and the Spirit of Yuma Festival are a few of the city's fun festivals.

The Colorado River is a favorite spot for swimming and fishing, and 14 golf courses are open year-round. Yuma also has some wildlife preserves, including the Yuma East Wetlands and the Imperial Sand Dunes.

Housing stock includes a lot of tract homes and gated communities, many of which spill into the desert. Dozens of RV parks dot the area.

Population: 93,000 (city proper)

Percentage of Population Age 45 or Better: 32%

Cost of Living: 7% below the national average

Median Home Price: $118,000

Climate: Summer high temperatures reach well into the 110s and last from May until September and October. Winters are mild and dry with temperatures in the 50s, 60s and 70s.

At Least One Hospital Accepts Medicare Patients? Yes

At Least One Hospital Accredited by Joint Commission? No, but the Ft. Yuma Phs Indian Hospital in Winterhaven, California, about 6 miles outside of Yuma, is accredited.

Public Transit: Yes

Crime Rate: Meets the national average

Public Library: Yes

Political Leanings: Conservative

Is Arizona Considered Tax Friendly for Retirement? Yes

Cons: The earthquake risk is 1,235% higher than the national average.

Notes: Marine Corps Air Station Yuma is located here, and jets fly over the city.

Arkansas

Fayetteville, Arkansas

Nestled in northwestern Arkansas' beautiful Ozark Mountains, easygoing Fayetteville receives great reviews all around. Rural, friendly and growing, it is home to the University of Arkansas (25,000 students) and has a Southern collegiate vibe.

The University is at the center of Fayetteville life, and Razorback athletics bring people in from around the region.   The city has landed on numerous "best places to live and retire" lists and enjoys a relatively low unemployment rate. This is thanks not only to UA but to Walmart, which has corporate partners based here.

The city has several distinct districts, including the charming Fayetteville Historic Square (the original center of town), College Avenue (which has lots of shops and restaurants) and Dickson Street (home to entertainment venues).

Nearby lakes, trails and rivers are perfect for all kinds of outdoor adventure. Festivals and events include the Fall Carnival and the Mud Fears Me 3K Run.

UA's Department of Fine Arts presents theater and music performances. The University also has an Osher Lifelong Learning Institute (OLLI) and a Road Scholar (Elderhostel) program.

Population: 74,000 (city proper)

Percentage of Population Age 45 or Better: 25%

Cost of Living: 8% below the national average

Median Home Price: $160,000

Climate: Fayetteville has a humid, four-season climate. Summer temperatures are in the 80s and 90s. Winters are mild, with temperatures in the 30s, 40s and 50s.

At Least One Hospital Accepts Medicare Patients? Yes

At Least One Hospital Accredited by Joint Commission? Yes

Public Transit: Yes, provided by Ozark Regional Transit

Crime Rate: Meets the national average

Public Library: Yes

Political Leanings: Conservative

Is Arkansas Considered Tax Friendly for Retirement? Yes

Cons: The tornado risk is 175% higher than the national average. The poverty rate is above the national average, but this is attributed to the large student population.

Notes: Fayetteville is a nice city with a lot to offer for the price.

Colorado

Grand Junction, Colorado

Grand Junction sits on a high desert plateau in western Colorado. It dates from the 1880s and has a history of cattle ranching, farming and energy exploration. Within the last decade, it has grown by 25% and today is home to Mesa University (9,000 students).

An unassuming, quiet place, Grand Junction has a mix of outdoor enthusiasts, families and retirees, as well as college kids. It is also known as a mountain biking hub, with riders coming from across the West to test their cycling skills on world-class mountain trails. Residents enjoy hiking and camping in nearby Colorado National Monument and rafting and fishing along the Colorado River and Gunnison River.

The downtown area is cozy and cute with outdoor restaurants, art galleries, sculptures, breweries and tree-lined streets. Mesa University's beautiful Moss Performing Arts Center hosts music and theater productions. Mesa Mall has J.C. Penney, Sears, Target and specialty stores.

Neighborhoods within town are typically suburban and well maintained with bungalows, ranch ramblers and raised ranch ramblers. Outside of town, beautiful homes are nestled in the scrub brush and rocky red terrain. Gorgeous Redlands Mesa is a master-planned development that has been called one of the world's most exceptional golf course communities. Another 7 golf courses are in and around town.

Population: 58,000 (city proper)

Percentage of Population Age 45 or Better: 40%

Cost of Living: Meets the national average

Median Home Price: $170,000

Climate: This area has a semi-arid to arid climate. Summer temperatures sometimes reach 100 degrees, and winter temperatures are in the teens, 20s and 30s. On average, the area receives 8 inches of rain and 20 inches of snow per year. The elevation is 4,640 feet above sea level.

At Least One Hospital Accepts Medicare Patients? Yes

At Least One Hospital Accredited by Joint Commission? Yes

Public Transit: Yes, and the city has a regional airport. Amtrak also has a station here.

Crime Rate: Meets the national average

Public Library: Yes

Political Leanings: Very conservative

Is Colorado Considered Tax Friendly for Retirement? Yes

Cons: None

Notes: Grand Junction sits along Interstate 70 but is somewhat isolated.

Florida

Beverly Beach, Florida

This tiny, tightly-knit Flagler County town sits on a barrier island between the Matanzas River and the Atlantic Ocean on Florida's northeastern coast. It is only 1.3 miles long and straddles scenic Highway A1A.

Primarily residential with a beautiful beach, Beverly Beach has older seaside homes and some condominiums. Surfside Estates is a large, compact mobile home park for people age 55 or better. A new, higher-end development named Sunset Inlet has 31 conch-style homes with riverside docks.

The local Herschel King Park has a riverside boat ramp and a canoe launch. Fishing is permitted on the beach and on the riverside seawall.

Camptown RV Resort sits between A1A and the ocean and has a general store. Most shopping and commercial services, though, are in Flagler Beach or Palm Coast, the town's next door neighbors.

Even though Beverly Beach is small, it has a mayor, commissioners and a town hall. Flagler Beach's senior center, which is just down the road, provides hot lunches, computer help and has a lending library.

Nearby attractions include the Graham Swamp Conservation Area and the Washington Oaks State Park. The centerpiece of Washington Oaks is a formal garden, but there are also short trails for hiking and biking.

Population: 350 (city proper)

Percentage of Population Age 45 or Better: 80%

Cost of Living: 5% below the national average

Median Home Price: $135,000

Climate: This area has a humid subtropical climate, meaning two seasons a year. Summer and early fall are hot and humid. Late fall and winter are less humid and cooler.

At Least One Hospital Accepts Medicare Patients? No, but Florida Hospital Flagler, 4 miles away in Palm Coast, accepts Medicare patients.

At Least One Hospital Accredited by Joint Commission?   No, but Florida Hospital Flagler, 4 miles away in Palm Coast, is accredited.

Public Transit: Flagler County Public Transportation has an on-demand van system that runs through the County.

Crime Rate: Below the national average

Public Library: No, but one is 3 miles away in Flagler Beach.

Political Leanings: Nearly split down the middle

Is Florida Considered Tax Friendly for Retirement?   Yes

Cons: The town is completely vulnerable if a hurricane should strike.

Notes: The RV resort is popular with "snowbirds." Taxes related to Sunset Inlet are helping increase town revenues. Beverly Beach has lost population, but the new Sunset Inlet is slowly helping to increase the number of residents.

Bushnell, Florida

Bushnell is the kind of place where everyone knows everyone else, and traditional values are cherished. It is not fancy or affluent, but it is closely knit and quiet, situated roughly equidistant between Tampa and Orlando in north central Florida.

In 1992, the town won Florida's Outstanding Rural Community Award, and not much has changed since then. Bushnell still has a country ambiance, with live oaks, weeping willows and two lane roads without sidewalks. Older concrete block homes, brick ranch ramblers and wood frame bungalows sit on large lots.

Residents enjoy a community center and 3 parks, but the Fall Festival is the town's main event and attracts 20,000 people. It features food, music, a parade and a greased pig catching contest.

The town center is simple but has a nice fountain and squat red and blond brick structures. Mom and pop retailers and government buildings dot the streets.

Nearby 80-acre Dade Battlefield Historic State Park preserves an 1835 battlefield where Seminole Indians and U.S. soldiers fought. It has an annual reenactment, as well as picnic tables and a nature trail.

Population: 2,500 (city proper)

Percentage of Population Age 45 or Better: 47%

Cost of Living: 10% below the national average

Median Home Price: $108,000

Climate: Bushnell has a humid, subtropical climate. Summer temperatures are in the 80s and 90s, and winter temperatures are in the 50s 60s and 70s. On average, the area receives 50 inches of rain per year.

At Least One Hospital Accepts Medicare Patients? No, but Leesburg Regional Medical Center, 17 miles away, accepts Medicare patients.

At Least One Hospital Accredited by Joint Commission? No, but

Leesburg Regional Medical Center, 17 miles away, is accredited.

Public Transit: The County provides a shuttle service within town.

Crime Rate: Meets the national average

Public Library: Yes

Political Leanings: Very conservative

Is Florida Considered Tax Friendly for Retirement? Yes

Cons: The tornado risk is 125% higher than the national average.

Notes: Residents seem to like Bushnell, and it has grown by 9% over the last decade. The town is home to the Sumter Correctional Institute, a facility for juvenile offenders. Interstate 75 runs just to the west of Bushnell, providing easy access to Tampa.

Cape Coral, Florida

Beautiful Cape Coral is west of Fort Myers on the southwestern Florida coast and sprang up in the 1950s as a master-planned community. It has been growing steadily ever since. In fact, thanks to its sprawling 114-square-mile borders, Cape Coral is the largest city between Tampa and Miami.

The city's 400 miles of canals comprise one of the largest canal systems in the world and create a soothing ambiance. Bays and sounds are all around, and opportunities for boating and fishing are abundant.

Residents enjoy two beaches, a handful of golf courses, numerous tennis courts, a water park and fishing piers. A community theater, a local art league and a fun farmers' market add to the quality of life. Shopping centers and some good restaurants are sprinkled around town.

The city hosts several festivals, including the Independence Day bash and Oktoberfest. The daddy of them all, though, is the huge Festival of the Arts, which draws 300 artists and 100,000 visitors each January.

The Parks and Recreation Department has a good menu of programs. Thanks to Cape Coral being mapped out from the beginning, bike paths, pedestrian walkways and parks are well designed and plentiful.

Homes range from stunning waterfront mansions to high rise condominiums. Many residences have a boat slip.

Population: 155,000 (city proper)

Percentage of Population Age 45 or Better: 45%

Cost of Living: 3% below the national average

Median Home Price: $150,000

Climate: Cape Coral has a hot, humid climate. Summer temperatures are in the 80s and 90s with high humidity levels and frequent rainstorms. Winter temperatures are in the 60s and 70s.

Public Transit: Yes, provided by LeeTran

At Least One Hospital Accepts Medicare Patients? Yes

At Least One Hospital Accredited by Joint Commission? Yes

Crime Rate: Below the national average

Public Library: Yes

Political Leanings: Conservative

Is Florida Considered Tax Friendly for Retirement? Yes

Cons: Cape Coral is home to the invasive Nile Monitor, a 9 foot long lizard that swims in the canals and eats small animals and fish. The area is susceptible to hurricanes and was struck by Hurricane Charley in 2004.

Notes: The city seems to lack cohesiveness but has landed on "best places to live" lists.

North Port, Florida

Originally established by the land development business General Development Company in the late-1950s, North Port straddles the Myakka River in southwestern Florida. It is about an hour north of Fort Myers and an hour and a half south of Tampa.

North Port is a fast growing place, having more than doubled in size during the last 10 years. Some of this growth has come through annexation of neighboring towns.

The city is suburban and leafy, nearly covered with meandering streets and planned residential neighborhoods that have a mix of young families and retirees. Homes are primarily ranch ramblers.

The part of town not covered by homes is to the southwest and across the river. Here the land gives way to the Myakka State Forest. Dense and lush, the forest is open for bicycling, bird watching, horseback riding, camping, fishing and hiking.

The city has an active parks and recreation department. One of its most popular events is Newcomer Welcome Days for people who have just relocated here or who are considering making the move.

The City Hall is attractive, but there is no real downtown. Merchants include grocery stores, bicycle repair shops, donut shops, a Saturday farmers' market and the like, but most services and shopping venues are in neighboring Charlotte.

Cultural opportunities are in good supply, though. The North Port Chorale has been entertaining residents since 1980. The North Port Symphony has reasonably priced season concert packages. The North Port Concert Band has a robust schedule and is composed of dedicated volunteers. The North Port Art Center has classes for all ages.

Population: 57,000 (city proper)

Percentage of Population Age 45 or Better: 45%

Cost of Living: 8% below the national average

Median Home Price: $130,000

Climate: This area has a humid subtropical climate, meaning two seasons a year. Summer and early fall are hot and humid. Late fall and winter are less humid and cooler.

At Least One Hospital Accepts Medicare Patients? No, but Fawcett Memorial Hospital, 9 miles away in Port Charlotte, accepts Medicare patients.

At Least One Hospital Accredited by Joint Commission? No, but Fawcett Memorial Hospital, 9 miles away in Charlotte, is accredited.

Public Transit: Yes

Crime Rate: Meets the national average

Public Library: Yes

Political Leanings: Conservative

Is Florida Considered Tax Friendly for Retirement? Yes

Cons: The tornado risk is 74% higher than the national average.

Notes: Warm Mineral Springs, located in North Port, is a sink hole that draws people hoping to be healed by its soothing, mineral-rich waters.

Palm Bay, Florida

Low key Palm Bay grew quickly during the 2004 to 2008 housing boom. The city is now the largest metropolis on Florida's Space Coast and is within 30 minutes of Port Canaveral, Florida's second busiest cruise port.

Originally settled at the mouth of Turkey Creek, Palm Bay is named after the sabal palms that grow here, and it is primarily a residential place. Although the city lacks a classic downtown, shopping centers and light industrial parks are scattered here and there.

A large community college campus, a community theater and 2 libraries are also here. Locally owned eateries and national restaurant chains serve everything from seafood to South American cuisine.

Turkey Creek wanders through town, and the Turkey Creek Sanctuary has a boardwalk, a nature center, canoe access points and a mountain bike trail. Wildlife in the Turkey Creek Sanctuary includes ospreys and manatees. Palm Bay's parks and recreation department sponsors an outdoor movie series and food truck wars.

The northeast and northwest areas of the city have older homes in established neighborhood. Newer residences, nicer neighborhoods, better roads and a somewhat rural quality are found in the city's southeast and southwest sections.

Population: 103,000 (city proper)

Percentage of Population Age 45 or Better: 35%

Cost of Living: 13% below the national average

Median Home Price: $95,000

Climate: This area has hot, humid summers and mild winters. Summer temperatures are in the 80s and 90s, and winter temperatures are in the 60s and 70s. On average, the area receives 50 inches of rain per year.

At Least One Hospital Accepts Medicare Patients? Yes

At Least One Hospital Accredited by Joint Commission? No, but Holmes Regional Medical Center, about 7 miles away in Melbourne, is accredited.

Public Transit: Yes

Crime Rate: Meets the national average

Public Library: Yes

Political Leanings: Conservative

Is Florida Considered Tax Friendly for Retirement? Yes

Cons: Managing the rapid growth has been an issue. Certain parts of town are less desirable than others. Much of the narrow beach is privately owned.

Notes: A housing dollar goes a long way here.

Palm Harbor, Florida

Pleasant, residential Palm Harbor is about 25 miles north of downtown Tampa on Florida's west central coast and is bounded by the Gulf of Mexico on the west and by 2,500-acre Lake Tarpon on the east. It dates from 1888 and today is well known as the home of the privately owned, world class Innisbrook Golf and Resort Club.

Although it is unincorporated, Palm Harbor has all of the earmarks of an incorporated town. Special tax districts pay for an active library and parks department. The historic district named Old Palm

Harbor is quiet but has little shops, sidewalk cafes and a pub or two.

Housing is a good mix of modest bungalows, ranch ramblers and exquisite, sand-colored Mediterranean-style estates. The western shore is lined with beautiful residences.

Boating and fishing opportunities are abundant, and Honeymoon Island State Park, which is accessible via the Dunedin Causeway, has 4 miles of beaches, mangrove swamps, tidal flats, a pine forest, nature trails and plenty of wildlife (hawks, alligators, snakes, etc.).

The chamber of commerce sponsors a wide variety of community events, including the First Friday celebration, the Citrus Festival and a beer fest. The Harbor Arts Festival has been in business for more than 30 years.

The Pop Stansell Park, on Sutherland Bayou, has a band shell and a marina, and the Palm Harbor Museum hosts a Saturday farmers' market. The city has 10 golf courses.

Population: 58,000 (city proper)

Percentage of Population Age 45 or Better: 47%

Cost of Living: 1% below the national average

Median Home Price: $165,000

Climate: Summer temperatures are in the 80s and 90s with high humidity levels and frequent rainstorms. Winter temperatures are in the 60s and 70s.

At Least One Hospital Accepts Medicare Patients? No, but Helen Ellis Memorial Hospital in Tarpon Springs, 5 miles away, accepts Medicare patients.

At Least One Hospital Accredited by Joint Commission? No, but

Helen Ellis Memorial Hospital in Tarpon Springs, 5 miles away, is accredited.

Public Transit: Yes

Crime Rate: Meets the national average

Public Library: Yes, and it has a good menu of programs and activities.

Political Leanings: Liberal

Is Florida Considered Tax Friendly for Retirement? Yes

Cons: The tornado risk is 90% greater than the national average.

Notes: The city is known for its excellent schools.

Riverview, Florida

Situated on the shores of the Alafia River on Florida's southwestern coast, Riverview is one of Tampa's unincorporated suburbs. It began in 1885 and grew slowly over the years. In the last 10 years, though, it has boomed and more than doubled in size.

The community has a lot of named neighborhoods and gated communities with attractive, relatively new Mediterranean-style homes. Doctor offices, grocery stores and big box stores are all close by, as are Sarasota and St. Pete Beach.

Hillsborough County operates more than 150 neighborhood parks, many of which are within Riverview's boundaries. Alafia Scrub Preserve and Bell Creek Preserve offer opportunities for hiking and nature study, and The Oaks at Riverview Senior Center sponsors "Let's Move!" walks.

The city has 7 golf courses, and 2 stunning state parks are in the neighborhood. Hillsborough River State Park has Class II rapids and kayak launches. Alafia River State Park, located on a former phosphate mining site, has some of the most radical elevation changes in Florida. Its off-road bike trails are particularly challenging. Canoeing and fishing are permitted on the Park's many lakes.

Population: 71,000 (city proper)

Percentage of Population Age 45 or Better: 58%

Cost of Living: 5% below the national average

Median Home Price: $145,000

Climate: Riverview has a humid, subtropical climate. Summer temperatures are in the 80s and 90s, and winter temperatures are in the 50s, 60s and 70s. On average, the area receives 55 inches of rain per year.

At Least One Hospital Accepts Medicare Patients? No, but Brandon Regional Hospital is 5 miles away and accepts Medicare patients.

At Least One Hospital Accredited by Joint Commission? No, but Brandon Regional Hospital is 5 miles away and is accredited.

Public Transit: Yes

Crime Rate: Below the national average

Public Library: Yes

Political Leanings: Liberal

Is Florida Considered Tax Friendly for Retirement? Yes

Cons: None, although some neighborhoods are less desirable than others.

Notes: One local legend claims that Riverview is haunted.

Ruskin, Florida

Unincorporated Ruskin sits along Tampa Bay and the Little Manatee River in a rural part of southwestern Florida. It is about half way between Tampa and Bradenton and was an agricultural center for most of its 100 or more years.

In the last decade, however, housing has sprung up, and Ruskin has nearly doubled in size. The primary draw is a mellow, country way of life near the water where crickets and frogs sing at night.

With inlets, islets and the rarely crowded river meandering on the south side of town, Ruskin is a good spot for fishing, kayaking and canoeing. The Cockroach Aquatic Bay Preserve, 4,800 acres of protected wetlands, has been restored and is a particular point of pride. Two more protected natural areas are to the northeast and southeast.

The Shellpoint Marina, situated at the mouth of the river, is not fancy but gets the job done. Ruskin is not known for its beaches because the small strip of sand belongs to the very nice Resort and Club at Little Harbor. So people in search of sand and sun travel 20 miles south to Bradenton or 6 miles north to Apollo Beach (which has clothing optional beaches).

Residents enjoy an organic market, the Ruskin Seafood and Arts Festival and the Ruskin Tomato Festival, as well as pretty views of St. Pete. Hillsborough Community College has classes for all ages. Shopping and services are limited.

Homes on the west side of town are older, and east side neighborhoods attract young families. Suburbs on the south have residences along the shore of Little Manatee River. Ruskin also backs to Sun City Center, a large 55+ community.

Population: 17,000 (city proper)

Percentage of Population Age 45 or Better: 37%

Cost of Living: 8% below the national average

Median Home Price: $130,000

Climate: Summer temperatures are in the 80s and 90s. Winter temperatures are in the 60s and 70s. On average, the area receives 55 inches of rain per year.

Public Transit: No

Crime Rate: Below the national average

Public Library: Yes

At Least One Hospital Accepts Medicare Patients? Yes

At Least One Hospital Accredited by Joint Commission? Yes

Political Leanings: Liberal

Is Florida Considered Tax Friendly for Retirement? Yes

Cons: The poverty rate is slightly above the national average.

Notes: The area has a large migrant farm worker population. Ruskin tried to incorporate in 2007 but failed to do so.

Tavares, Florida

Located in north central Florida, about 30 miles outside of Orlando, semi-rural Tavares bills itself as "America's Seaplane City." It borders 4 large lakes and has several other smaller bodies of water within its boundaries.

Water events and activities abound and include cypress swamp eco-cruises, a bass fishing tournament, a race boat regatta, an antique boat show, a dragon boat show, Jet Ski races and many more. Seaplane fly-ins attract pilots from around the region and feature contests with awards for such things as "shortest take off" and "best spot landing."

The city-owned, 40-slip Seaplane Base and Marina is in the simple but attractive downtown. Wooten Park, along Lake Dora and close to the town center, has a popular water park and huge live oaks with dripping moss.

The downtown is also the site of the Tuesday morning farmers' market. Residents have a few restaurants from which to choose, but shopping venues are limited.

A lot of neighborhoods are modest with older concrete block homes and ranch ramblers. Tavares is growing, however, so there are also new subdivisions with modern home designs. Many residences, new and old, are located on a lake or in a lakeside community with water access.

Population: 14,000 (city proper)

Percentage of Population Age 45 or Better: 60%

Cost of Living: 6% below the national average

Median Home Price: $124,000

Climate: Tavares has a humid subtropical climate with an average 48 inches of rainfall each year. Summer temperatures are in the 80s and 90s, and winters are mild with temperatures in the 50s, 60s and 70s.

At Least One Hospital Accepts Medicare Patients? Yes

At Least One Hospital Accredited by Joint Commission? Yes

Public Transit: Yes

Crime Rate: Below the national average

Public Library: Yes

Political Leanings: Conservative

Is Florida Considered Tax Friendly for Retirement? Yes

Cons: The tornado risk is 126% higher than the national average.

Notes: Tavares is a nice town.

Georgia

Athens, Georgia

Leafy Athens is located in northeastern Georgia, about 75 miles east of Atlanta. It is a quintessential college town and home to the sprawling University of Georgia (35,000 students), one of the oldest state-chartered schools in the country.

Nicknamed the "Classic City" because many of its buildings were inspired by classic Greek architecture, Athens boasts an intact 19th-century cityscape and is this region's cultural and health care hub. Residents enjoy a creative, trendy vibe combined with mellow, Southern charm.

The city's distinct neighborhoods are full of character, and 14 of them are listed on the National Register of Historic Places. Architectural styles include Greek Revival as well as Italianate, American Foursquare, Craftsman, Tutor Revival and nearly 25 more.

The University (UGA) campus dominates Athens and ensures that there is always something engaging to do. The Hugh Hodgson School of Music presents 300 performances per year, and all are open to the public. The Georgia Museum of Art and the Lamar Dodd School of Art both have permanent and rotating exhibits. The UGA Performing Arts Center has a rich schedule and hosts the Atlanta Symphony Orchestra. On autumn weekends, the population swells as fans flock to University of Georgia football games.

The thriving downtown is a fun area with shops, pubs, art galleries and music venues. Jazz, blues and rock bands perform on club stages every night of the week. The city has 500 restaurants, several of which are award-winning.

Strolling through the State Botanical Garden is a wonderful way to spend an afternoon. Memorial Park has hiking trails and green spaces.

Population: 115,000 (city proper)

Percentage of Population Age 45 or Better: 25%

Cost of Living: 2% below the national average

Median Home Price: $160,000

Climate: Summers temperatures are in the 80s and 90s, and winter temperatures are in the 30s, 40s and 50s. On average, the area receives 50 inches of rain and a dusting of snow each year

At Least One Hospital Accepts Medicare Patients? Yes

At Least One Hospital Accredited by Joint Commission? Yes

Public Transit: Yes

Crime Rate: Below the national average

Public Library: Yes

Political Leanings: Liberal

Is Georgia Considered Tax Friendly for Retirement? Yes

Cons: UGA has a reputation as a party school. The poverty rate is above the national average, although much of this is attributed to the large student population.

Notes: The University sponsors the 1,000-member Osher Lifelong Learning Institute (OLLI), an organization that offers a wide selection of classes and workshops to people age 50 or better.

St. Marys, Georgia

Along the St. Marys River on Georgia's southern coast, about six miles from the Atlantic Ocean, the charming coastal village of St. Marys makes its home. It dates from the late-1700s and has been a fishing port, a lumber processing hub and a paper mill town.

Today, while fishing is still important, the economy is largely based on the U.S. military and tourism. Naval Submarine Base Kings Bay, a Trident submarine base, is right next door, and the Cumberland Island National Seashore, accessible only by boat, is just across the Cumberland Sound.

Neighborhoods are leafy, and housing is a mixture of the modest and the extraordinary. Some areas have simple brick residences set on smaller lots while others contain palatial estates along the water. Osprey Cove is a beautiful 55+ development with a championship golf course and water access. Military families are sprinkled throughout town.

With a sleepy harbor and sweeping marsh views, St. Marys exudes tranquility. At the waterfront, shrimp boats are moored along the dock as they have been since the early days, and private pleasure vessels come and go in a leisurely fashion.

Shopping choices include specialty shops, boutiques and major retailers, including Walmart, J.C. Penny and Belk. The St. Marys Community Market, an open air farmers' market, takes place every

Saturday year-round. Restaurants include some national chains, as well as locally owned cafes and diners.

Mardi Gras, the Rock Shrimp Festival, Hays Days and Christmas in the Park all bring out sizeable crowds. Three museums, including the Greek Revival Orange House Hall Museum, a testament to antebellum life, are fun places to spend an afternoon. St. Marys Little Theater has an engaging, year-round schedule.

Jekyll Island and Fernandina Beach are both close by and have pretty, public beaches. Cumberland Island National Seashore, the reason many people come to St. Marys, has a federally-protected, unspoiled shoreline where wild hogs and feral horses roam freely. This is the place to hike, kayak, gather seashells or watch the stars.

Population: 17,000 (city proper)

Percentage of Population Age 45 or Better: 20%

Cost of Living: 7% below the national average

Median Home Price: $140,000

Climate: Summer temperatures are in the 70s, 80s and 90s, and winter temperatures are usually in the 50s and 60s. On average, the area receives 50 inches of rain each year.

At Least One Hospital Accepts Medicare Patients? Yes

At Least One Hospital Accredited by Joint Commission? Yes

Public Transit: No

Crime Rate: Meets the national average

Public Library: Yes

Political Leanings: Conservative

Is Georgia Considered Tax Friendly for Retirement? Yes

Cons: This is an old town, and parts of the infrastructure are outdated.   Some areas flood during intense rain storms.   Traffic congestion is an issue during tourist season.

Notes: St. Marys has grown by 20% within the last decade.

Idaho

Idaho Falls, Idaho

Quiet, welcoming Idaho Falls often lands on "best places to live" lists.   It sits along the Snake River in eastern Idaho and started out as an agricultural community in the late-1800s.   A clean, well-tended city, it serves as a hub not only for eastern Idaho but also for western Wyoming.

A beautiful greenbelt meanders along the river, and the downtown has a nice mix of trendy shops, established retailers and office buildings. It is also home to a Saturday's farmers' market, art shows and concerts.

The city's neighborhoods are not clearly defined, but the original section of town on the east side of the river has homes from the 1930s, 1940s and 1950s.   Neighborhoods on the west side of the water date from the 1960s and continue to grow. New retail and residential centers include Taylors Crossing and Snake River Landing.

Residents enjoy the Tautphaus Park Zoo, the Idaho Falls Symphony, the Repertory Artists' Theatre, the Willard Arts Center and the historic Colonial Theatre, which hosts music and theater performances.

Outdoor recreation beckons at every turn, with fishing along the river particularly popular. Yellowstone National Park and Grand Teton National Park are just two hours away by car.

Population: 57,000 (city proper)

Percentage of Population Age 45 or Better: 32%

Cost of Living: 8% below the national average

Median Home Price: $140,000

Climate: Idaho Falls sits at 4,700 feet above sea level and has 4 seasons. Winters usually bring temperatures in the teens, 20s and 30s, and summers are cool with temperatures in the 60s, 70s and low-80s. On average, the area receives 12 inches of rain and 30 inches of snow per year.

At Least One Hospital Accepts Medicare Patients? Yes

At Least One Hospital Accredited by Joint Commission? Yes

Public Transit: Yes, provided by Targhee Regional Transportation Authority

Crime Rate: Meets the national average

Public Library: Yes

Political Leanings: Very, very conservative

Is Idaho Considered Tax Friendly for Retirement? Yes

Cons: The earthquake risk is 230% above the national average.

Notes: The city has a large Church of Jesus Christ of Latter Day Saints population. A recent university study found Idaho Falls to be the second happiest city in the U.S. (Napa, California was found to be the happiest).

Iowa

Ankeny, Iowa

Appealing Ankeny is a tidy suburb about 10 miles north of Des Moines and 6 miles east of Saylorville Lake in pastoral central Iowa. It has been growing very fast, increasing its population by nearly 70% in the last decade. It is a wholesome, family-oriented place with good public schools. Residents seem to love living here.

Neighborhoods are prim, and housing stock includes wood frame bungalows, brick ranch ramblers and raised ranch ramblers. New gated communities are here, too, and the extended parks system ensures that nearly every home is within walking distance of a grassy green space.

The attractive downtown, called Uptown, is dotted with awning-draped merchants. Shopping choices include national retailers, locally owned boutiques and a farmers' market. The city is home to biotech firms and manufacturing companies, including John Deere, the town's largest employer.

Des Moines Area Community College has classes for all ages. The Ankeny Art Center, the Ankeny Community Chorus and the Ankeny Community Theatre add a bit of culture.

Saylorville Lake covers 6,000 acres and is a popular place for boating and fishing. The two adjacent state parks have camping grounds and hiking trails.

Population: 45,000 (city proper)

Percentage of Population Age 45 or Better: 30%

Cost of Living: 5% below the national average

Median Home Price: $165,000

Climate: This area has a humid continental climate, meaning hot, humid summers and cold, snowy winters. Summer temperatures are in the 80s and 90s, and winter temperatures range from below 0 to the 20s. On average, Ankeny receives 30 inches of rain each and 25 inches of snow each year.

At Least One Hospital Accepts Medicare Patients? No, but Des Moines has several hospitals that accept Medicare patients.

At Least One Hospital Accredited by Joint Commission? No, but Des Moines has several hospitals that are accredited.

Public Transit: Yes, provided by Ankeny Express, but it only makes a few stops in town and then heads to Des Moines.

Crime Rate: Meets the national average

Public Library: Yes

Political Leanings: Liberal

Is Iowa Considered Tax Friendly for Retirement? No

Cons: The air quality is slightly below the national average, and the tornado risk is 215% greater than the national average.

Notes: Ankeny has landed on "best places to live" lists.

Kentucky

Elizabethtown, Kentucky

Friendly, well-maintained Elizabethtown, or E-town as it is called locally, got its start in 1793 and sits along the old North Dixie Highway (Highway 31W) and Interstate 65 in rural north central Kentucky. It is about 12 miles south of Fort Knox, the military base where the U.S. Bullion Depository is located. Thanks to this locale, many military personnel live in Elizabethtown.

Established neighborhoods are generally modest with wood frame ranch ramblers, while newer areas have spacious brick homes on larger lots. The historic town core is simple but attractive with brick buildings that house shops, government offices, attorneys, museums and eateries.

Elizabethtown is proud of its heritage and has numerous Civil War and military attractions, including the (George) Patton Museum and Confederate Cemetery Hill. Residents also enjoy historic house walking tours, a community theater, touring shows at the performing arts center and a quilt trail.

Fun festivals include October's Ghost Walk, the Christmas Parade and November's Light Up Downtown. Walking trails meander around town, and Freeman Lake Park has fishing and picnic areas. Elizabethtown Community and Technical College has classes for all ages.

Some very good locally owned restaurants complement national chains. A farmers' market has fresh produce and dairy items. Six shopping centers and a mall line busy Highway 31W.

Population: 29,000 (city proper)

Percentage of Population Age 45 or Better: 37%

Cost of Living: 10% below the national average

Median Home Price: $135,000

Climate: Summer temperatures are in the 80s and 90s. Winter temperatures are in the 20s, 30s and 40s. On average, the area receives 50 inches of rain and 3 inches of snow per year.

At Least One Hospital Accepts Medicare Patients? Yes

At Least One Hospital Accredited By Joint Commission? Yes

Public Transit: The County has an on-demand van service. People age 60 or better ride for free, although a donation is requested.

Crime Rate: Meets the national average

Public Library: Yes

Political Leanings: Very conservative

Is Kentucky Considered Tax Friendly for Retirement? Yes

Cons: The air quality is below the national average, and the tornado risk is 127% higher than the national average.

Notes: E-town has grown by 24% in the last decade and has a reputation as a quiet, pleasant community. Louisville is 50 miles to the north via I-65.

Morehead, Kentucky

Nestled amid the deciduous trees of the Daniel Boone National Forest in eastern Kentucky's Appalachian Mountains, cozy Morehead is a small place with a big heart. It is the site of Morehead State University, which has more students (9,000) than the town has residents.

This situation gives Morehead a youthful energy and provides residents with plenty of things to do, including attending college football games, music performances and dance recitals. MSU's continuing education program has classes for the Morehead community.

The University's well-regarded Kentucky Folk Arts Center sponsors a number of annual events, including the A Day in the Country Folk Art Festival and the Autumn Arts and Eats Festival.   Other events include the Poppy Mountain Bluegrass Festival, the Cave Run Storytelling Festival and weekly noon outdoor concerts. Morehead Theatre Guild presents theater productions year-round.

Daniel Boone National Forest surrounds Morehead and provides opportunities for camping, fishing, and hiking. Nearby Cave Run Lake is the place for boating.

Neighborhoods have a country feeling. Homes are mostly ranch ramblers and raised ranch ramblers.

Population: 6,900 (city proper)

Percentage of Population Age 45 or Better: 30%

Cost of Living: 11% below the national average

Median Home Price: $125,000

Climate: Summer temperatures are in the 70s, 80s and 90s. Winter temperatures are in the 20s, 30s and 40s. On average, the area receives 44 inches of rain and 7 inches of snow per year.

At Least One Hospital Accepts Medicare Patients? Yes

At Least One Hospital Accredited by Joint Commission? Yes

Public Transit: Yes

Crime Rate: Below the national average

Public Library: Yes

Political Leanings: Split down the middle

Is Kentucky Considered Tax Friendly for Retirement? Yes

Cons: Morehead has a poverty rate above the national average, but much of this is attributed to the large student population.

Notes: Church attendance is very high. The city sits along Interstate 64, allowing easy access to Lexington to the west.

Murray, Kentucky

Surrounded by gently rolling hills and flat farm land in rural western Kentucky, Murray is a pleasant place that is home to Murray State University (11,000 students). It is also just 20 minutes from Land Between the Lakes, a huge recreation area with 2 lakes and 4,000 miles of shoreline.

In addition to bountiful lake recreation, residents enjoy 2 large parks, numerous tennis courts and 2 golf courses, one of which has been named as one of the best designed courses in America.

Murray also has its share of cultural amenities, including Playhouse in the Park, the Clara M. Eagle Gallery and the Wrather West Kentucky Museum. Lovett Live is a program that lets residents meet touring musical artists, and the Murray Art Guild has classes and workshops.

MSU has a good menu of lectures, theater performances and athletic events. Its basketball games are particularly popular. The University also offers free tuition to anyone age 65 or better.

Shopping venues include locally owned retailers and a J.C. Penney. A farmers' market and 75 churches are here, too.

New subdivisions mingle with older neighborhoods, and many residences are brick ranch ramblers.

Population: 18,000 (city proper)

Percentage of Population Age 45 or Better: 32%

Cost of Living: 13% below the national average

Median Home Price: $120,000

Climate: Summer temperatures are in the 80s and 90s, and winter temperatures are in the 30s and 40s. On average, the area receives 55 inches of rain and 9 inches of snow each year.

At Least One Hospital Accepts Medicare Patients? Yes

At Least One Hospital Accredited by Joint Commission? Yes

Public Transit: Yes, but it is limited.

Crime Rate: Well below the national average

Public Library: Yes

Political Leanings: Conservative

Is Kentucky Considered Tax Friendly for Retirement? Yes

Cons: The tornado risk is 153% greater than the national average. The poverty rate is well above the national average, but much of this is attributed to the large student population.

Notes: MSU does not have a reputation as a party school. Some people say that Murray can be a little cool to newcomers, while others say it is a friendly place. The senior center has a good reputation. Murray has grown by 14% in the last decade.

Mississippi

Hernando, Mississippi

Hernando, named after Spanish explorer Hernando de Soto, is a rapidly growing town about 25 miles south of Memphis, Tennessee. It is home to a sizeable musician population and has been landing on "best places to live" lists in the last few years. Its strong public school system, low unemployment rate and well-managed growth are a few reasons why.

The town dates from the early-1800s, and it takes pride in its heritage. Nicely maintained historic districts with grand antebellum homes stand side by side with modern suburbs, many of which only date from 1990.

The leafy town center is anchored by the stately red brick courthouse and is where the community meets for outdoor movies and festivals. The weekly farmers' market, also held here, has been named Mississippi's best farmers' market.

Hernando has been recognized for its efforts to promote healthy living, including developing a community garden, installing bicycle lanes and requiring that new neighborhoods be walkable. A city recycling program is in place, and new real estate developments must set aside land for open space.

New locally owned restaurants have been popping up, and at least one has garnered national attention. The De Soto Arts Council has a gallery, exhibits and classes, and the Kudzu Playhouse is a thriving community theater.

Population: 14,500 (city proper)

Percentage of Population Age 45 or Better: 34%

Cost of Living: 4% below the national average

Median Home Price: $185,000

Climate: On average, the area receives 50 inches of rain and 10 inches of snow annually. Summer temperatures are in the 80s and 90s, and winter temperatures are in the 20s, 30s and 40s.

Public Transit: No

Crime Rate: Well below the national average

Public Library: Yes

At Least One Hospital Accepts Medicare Patients? No, but Baptist Memorial Hospital in Southaven, about 10 miles to the north, accepts Medicare patients.

At Least One Hospital Accredited by Joint Commission? No, but Baptist Memorial Hospital in Southaven, about 10 miles to the north, is accredited and is a teaching hospital.

Political Leanings: Very conservative

Is Mississippi Considered Tax Friendly for Retirement? Somewhat

Cons: The tornado risk is 175% greater than the national average.

Notes: Hernando has doubled in size since the year 2000 but is still partly rural. Many residents commute to Memphis for work. What cannot be found in Hernando can be found in Southaven, 10 miles away, or in Memphis.

Nevada

Fallon, Nevada

Situated in a green landscape of cantaloupe fields, alfalfa crops and grazing cattle about an hour east of Reno, quiet Fallon sits along Highway 50, the "Loneliest Highway in America." Although the town is located in an arid region, it receives irrigation water from 2 lakes and a river, giving it the nickname the "Oasis of Nevada."

The downtown is simple but well maintained with wide streets, one and two story buildings, a few trees, mom and pop retailers and street parking. Residents enjoy a handful of casual casinos, and slot machines are found in restaurants and diners.

The Tuesday night farmers' market brings people out for delicious fresh food. The town honors its agricultural heritage by hosting Tractors and Truffles, a fun farm to table culinary event.

A motor speedway and a thriving County museum are here, too. The Naval Air Station Fallon is where elite fighter pilots are trained.

The Oats Park Arts Center is a town highlight. With its galleries, exhibitions and world-class performances, Oak Park draws audiences from Reno and Northern California.

The Lahontan Reservoir, about 20 miles outside of town, is popular with fishermen, boaters and campers. The nearby National Wildlife Refuge attracts hundreds of thousands of shorebirds during migration season.

Homes are mostly ranch ramblers and raised ranch ramblers.

Population: 8,600 (city proper)

Percentage of Population 45 or Better: 32%

Cost of Living: 5% below the national average

Median Home Price: $143,000

Climate: With an elevation of 3,965 feet above sea level, summer temperatures are in the 80s and 90s. Winter temperatures are in the teens, 20s and 30s. On average, the area receives 5 inches of rain and 5 inches of snow per year.

Public Transit: No

Crime Rate: Below the national average

Public Library: Yes

At Least One Hospital Accepts Medicare Patients? Yes

At Least One Hospital Accredited By Joint Commission? Yes

Political Leanings: Very conservative

Is Nevada Considered Tax Friendly for Retirement? Yes

Cons: Fallon is isolated. Reno is 62 miles away, and Interstate 80 is about 50 miles to the north. The earthquake risk is 498% greater than the national average.

Notes: The Truckee - Carson Irrigation District taps the nearby Lahontan Reservoir for irrigation purposes, so the lake is often half empty by September. Fallon has grown by 7% in the last decade.

Laughlin, Nevada

Located on the Colorado River in southern Nevada, Laughlin was once nothing more than a dusty, desert outpost. Today, it is a gambling resort, with 9 lavish hotels and casinos, and it attracts 3 million vacationers per year.

These tourists come not only to gamble but to attend shows, get spa treatments and enjoy boating, water skiing and rafting on the river (which has a nice river walk). The Big Bend State Recreation Area just south of town is the place for fishing, camping, hiking and mountain biking. Mohave Resort Desert Club has 18 holes of golf.

Festivals include the Laughlin International Film Festival, the International Gift and Craft Show and the Laughlin Veterans' Festival. The city also hosts the annual Laughlin River Run, a motorcycle event that can bring 70,000 people to town over a 4 day period.

Laughlin Outlet Center has more than 60 retailers, and all the casinos have specialty shops. Dining options include national chain restaurants and casino eateries.

Housing stock consists primarily of Mediterranean-style ranch ramblers and raised ranch ramblers. Most residences have Xeriscaping.

Population: 7,500 (city proper)

Percentage of Population Age 45 or Better: 53%

Cost of Living: 9% below the national average

Median Home Price: $120,000

Climate: Summers are long with temperatures in the 90s and low-100s. Winters are dry and mild, with temperatures in the 50s, 60s and 70s. On average, the area receives 5 inches of rain per year.

At Least One Hospital Accepts Medicare Patients? No, but the Western Arizona Regional Medical Center, 4 miles south in Bullhead City, Arizona, accepts Medicare patients.

At Least One Hospital Accredited by Joint Commission? No, but the Western Arizona Regional Medical Center, 4 miles south in Bullhead City, Arizona, is accredited.

Public Transit: Yes, provided by Southern Nevada Transit

Crime Rate: Meets the national average

Public Library: Yes. The Laughlin Library is a beautiful building on a bluff overlooking the town and has 15,000 square feet, art exhibits and free wireless internet.

Political Leanings: Liberal

Is Nevada Considered Tax Friendly for Retirement? Yes

Cons: The air quality is below the national average.

Notes: Despite being a gambling town, Laughlin is clean and relatively quiet.

North Carolina

Asheboro, North Carolina

Located in the heart of the Uwharrie Mountains in the middle of North Carolina, attractive Asheboro has been growing. It dates from 1780 and in recent years has been recognized for its historic preservation and good government.

For much of the latter-20th century, Asheboro was a manufacturing hub, producing batteries, shoes and furniture. Its profile began to change in 1979 when the state-owned North Carolina Zoo opened. This 2,200-acre facility is the largest walk-through zoo in the world, home to 1,100 animals. It draws 700,000 visitors per year.

Local museums include a classic motorcycle gallery and an aviation hall of fame. Residents also enjoy the community Sunset Theater, 5 golf courses, a downtown farmers' market and a collegiate baseball team. Randolph Mall is small but has a Belk and a J.C. Penney.

The continuing education program at Randolph Community College offers classes in pottery and photography. The Randolph Arts Guild sponsors lectures, afternoon teas and trips.

Asheboro's downtown is simple but well maintained. Neighborhoods have a country quality with ranch ramblers on wooded lots.

Lake Reese has a kayak launch, and the city has an outdoor community pool and a tennis center. Lake Lucas boasts a fishing pier and boat rentals. The nearby Birkhead Mountains Wilderness Area is a popular hiking destination.

Population: 25,000 (city proper)

Percentage of Population 45 or Better: 35%

Cost of Living: 12% below the national average

Median Home Price: $100,000

Climate: Summer temperatures are in the 80s and 90s, and winter temperatures are in the 30s and 40s. On average, the area receives 45 inches of rain and 6 inches of snow per year.

At Least One Hospital Accepts Medicare Patients? Yes

At Least One Hospital Accredited By Joint Commission? Yes

Public Transit: No

Crime Rate: Below the national average

Public Library: Yes

Political Leanings: Very, very conservative

Is North Carolina Considered Tax Friendly for Retirement? Somewhat

Cons: The poverty rate meets the national average.

Notes: Residents seem to enjoy Asheboro very much.

Calabash, North Carolina

Calabash is a quaint fishing village with a long history and a nice reputation. It sits near the mouth of the quiet, crook-necked Calabash River where it joins the Intracoastal Waterway in southeastern North Carolina. The southernmost coastal town in the state, it is known as the "Seafood Capital of the World."

During the fishing season, boats dock daily in the oak-shaded port and sell shrimp to local restaurants that specialize in "Calabash-style" fried seafood. Four of these restaurants sit along the mellow waterfront. Charter boats stand by for tours and deep-sea fishing.

Peanut and indigo plantations once populated the surrounding land, and modern farms still sell pick-your-own strawberries and blueberries. In fact, Indigo Farms has a year-round market and garden center.

Although shopping in Calabash is limited, the adjoining town of Carolina Shores has a shopping center and a major grocery store.

Calabash is in a way two towns, an older part with smaller homes, many made from brick, and a newer section with several planned communities that cater to baby boomers and retirees. These include Crow Creek, Brunswick Plantation, the Village at Calabash and Savannah Lakes.

Thirty golf courses within thirty minutes and include the Brunswick Plantation and Golf Resort, which has three courses alone. Calabash is on the edge of North Carolina's busy Grand Strand and is less than hour from Myrtle Beach. For the sand and surf lovers, Sunset Beach, North Carolina is five miles away and has beaches.

Population: 2,100 (city proper)

Percentage of Population Age 45 or Better: 65%

Cost of Living: 2% below the national average

Median Home Price: $150,000

Climate: Summer temperatures are in the 80s and 90s, and winter temperatures are in 40s, 50s and 60s. On average, the receives 52 inches of rain per year.

At Least One Hospital Accepts Medicare Patients? No, but Grand Strand Regional Medical Center, 16 miles away in Myrtle Beach, accepts Medicare patients.

At Least One Hospital Accredited by the Joint Commission? No, but Grand Strand Regional Medical Center, 16 miles away in Myrtle Beach, is accredited.

Public Transit: No

Crime Rate: Well below the national average

Public Library: Yes

Political Leanings: Conservative

Is North Carolina Considered Tax Friendly for Retirement? Somewhat

Cons: Hurricanes are always a possibility.

Notes: Calabash has grown by 40% within the last decade.

Tryon, North Carolina

Quaint and artsy, Tryon is nestled in rural southwestern North Carolina's Blue Ridge Mountains and is surrounded by vineyards, orchards and waterfalls. It has a rich equestrian culture, too.

Only locally owned shops are allowed within city limits, and the small town core is well maintained.

The Tryon Fine Arts Center supports film shows, music events and visual arts, and the Tryon Arts and Crafts School houses professional studios. Its classes cover anything from blacksmithing to woodworking.

Tryon produces a beer festival, a music festival, and a Barbecue and Music Festival that receives rave reviews. The member-run Lanier Library hosts a poetry festival and is the oldest local civic organization.

The town's active riding and hunt club sponsors races, shows and clinics. The Foothills Equestrian Nature Center has a pond and trails for riding and bird watching. Harmon Field has four riding rings, 140 horse stalls, and a community garden.

Hiking is popular along the Pacelot River Byway and in the Norman Wilder Forest.

Many homes sit on thickly wooded country lots.

Population: 1,700 (city proper)

Percentage of Population Age 45 or Better: 58%

Cost of Living: 2% below the national average

Median Home Price: $160,000

Climate: Summer temperatures are in 80s and 90s, and winter temperatures are in 30s and 40s. On average, the area receives 64 inches of rain and 5 inches of snow per year. The elevation is 1,050 feet above sea level.

At Least One Hospital Accepts Medicare Patients? No, but St. Luke's Hospital is 5 miles away in Columbus and accepts Medicare patients.

At Least One Hospital Accredited by the Joint Commission? No, but St. Luke's Hospital, 5 miles away in Columbus, is accredited.

Public Transit: The County has a call ahead van service, and it is free for people age 60 or better.

Crime Rate: Meets the national average

Public Library: Yes

Political Leanings: Very conservative

Is North Carolina Considered Tax Friendly for Retirement?
Somewhat

Cons: Winter driving can be a little treacherous.

Notes: This is a pretty but remote area, although Tryon is accessible via Interstate 26 and a side road. The town has grown by 2% within the last decade. The air quality is outstanding.

Oklahoma

Norman, Oklahoma

Named after a surveyor in the 1889 Oklahoma Land Rush, pleasant Norman is in central Oklahoma and is home to the University of Oklahoma (30,000 students). It is a comfortable, growing Midwestern city and has landed on "best places to live" lists. Residents are an educated bunch.

The heart and soul of Norman is the University (OU), which is known for its top-rated football program. Loyalty to the OU Sooners runs deeply, and rivalries with the University of Texas, the University of Nebraska and Oklahoma State University are particularly intense.

OU also plays a large part in the city's scientific and cultural life. The National Weather Center is based here, and the well-regarded Fred Jones Jr. Museum of Art has 7 separate collections. The beautiful Donald W. Reynolds Performing Arts Center has the ambiance of a turn-of-the-century European concert hall. OU's theater and dance departments perform regularly.

The Norman Arts Council sponsors music festivals, open studios and writing workshops, and the city supports a ballet company and a philharmonic orchestra. The numerous city events include a Mardi Gras, a Medieval fair, an arts fair and music celebrations.

Lake Thunderbird State Park is in town, and its Lake Thunderbird has 86 miles of shoreline, 9 boat launches, a marina and a swimming beach. The park also has horse stables and primitive camping sites. The city's recreation department manages a good variety of parks, pools, golf courses and service centers.

Neighborhoods are leafy. Homes are mostly brick ranch ramblers and raised ranch ramblers.

Population: 112,000 (city proper)

Percentage of Population Age 45 or Better: 30%

Cost of Living: 10% below the national average

Median Home Price: $135,000

Climate: Summer temperatures are in the 80s and 90s, and winter temperatures are in the 20s, 30s and 40s. On average, the area receives 35 inches of rain and 6 inches of snow per year. Winters are often overcast.

At Least One Hospital Accepts Medicare Patients? Yes

At Least One Hospital Accredited by the Joint Commission? No. Norman Regional Hospital has a good reputation and is a Primary Stroke Center, but it is not accredited. Oklahoma City, 15 miles away, has accredited hospitals.

Public Transit: Yes

Crime Rate: Below the national average

Public Library: Yes

Political Leanings: Conservative

Is Oklahoma Considered Tax Friendly for Retirement? Yes

Cons: Norman is in "Tornado Alley" and has a tornado risk that is 420% higher than the national average. Traffic congestion is a problem, particularly on football weekends.

Notes: Some people say that the University has too much influence. OU has an OLLI (Osher Lifelong Learning Institute) for people age 50 and better. A lot of bars and clubs are near the main campus, particularly on the north side (Campus Corner). College nightlife is lively.

Oregon

Florence, Oregon

Florence is a scenic, slightly rustic waterfront town at the mouth of the Siuslaw River on Oregon's mid-coast. It is a popular place with retirees and has grown by 20% in the last 10 years. Commercial fishing has always played a part in this area's economy. It still does, but in recent years tourism and gambling have become just as important.

The Three Rivers Casino has 5 restaurants, nationally known entertainment acts, table games and 700 slot machines. Old Town is the touristy section along the river and has art galleries, bookstores, cafes and trinket stores. Shopping is not outstanding but good enough to cover the basics.

The annual Rhododendron Festival dates from 1908 and is a town highlight. While it is popular, a book festival, an arts festival and a dozen other festivals have fans, too. The Florence Events Center hosts exhibits, food and beer events, the Eugene Ballet and more.

Three state parks are nearby, and outdoor recreation plays a large part in many people's lives here. The stunning coastline is often dotted with walkers, photographers and beach combers.

Neighborhoods are wooded with ranch ramblers. Many homes have views of the water.

Population: 8,600 (city proper)

Percentage of Population Age 45 or Better: 62%

Cost of Living: 2% below the national average

Median Home Price: $155,000

Climate: Summers are cool with temperatures in the 50s, 60s and 70s. Winters are damp and even cooler, with temperatures in the 30s and 40s. Days are often overcast. On average, the area receives 76 inches of rain per year. Snow is rare.

At Least One Hospital Accepts Medicare Patients? Yes

At Least One Hospital Accredited by the Joint Commission? Yes

Public Transit: Yes, provided by Rhody Express

Crime Rate: Well below the national average

Public Library: Yes, and it has an interlibrary loan program, a vision enhancement machine and free wireless internet.

Political Leanings: Liberal

Is Oregon Considered Tax Friendly for Retirement? No

Cons: Winters are dreary. The closest city of any size is Eugene, 45 minutes to the east.

Notes: Peace Harbor Hospital is a Level IV adult trauma center.

Pennsylvania

Jim Thorpe, Pennsylvania

Beautiful Jim Thorpe, known as the "Switzerland of America," is nestled along the Lehigh River in rolling eastern Pennsylvania and has been hailed as a great little town by numerous national publications.

A gateway to the scenic Pocono Mountains, Jim Thorpe started out with the name Mauch Chunk, a Native American term for "sleeping bear." The name changed in 1953 when the widow of renowned athlete Jim Thorpe convinced the struggling coal hamlet to buy her husband's remains and erect a monument in his honor. She also requested that the town rename itself Jim Thorpe.

These days, Jim Thorpe's legacy brings a lot of tourists to town but so does the abundant outdoor recreation. Whitewater rafting, in particular, is top notch.

Shopping is mostly of the specialty type, but a general store has basic supplies. Restaurants range from the elegant to the casual.

The town's extraordinary architecture, a compact mix of Federal, Greek Revival, Second Empire, Romanesque Revival, Queen Anne and Richardsonian Romanesque, creates a wonderfully elegant cityscape. Many in-town homes date from the 1800s, while more contemporary dwellings, including raised ranch ramblers and cabins, are nestled in the woods.

Population: 4,800 (city proper)

Percentage of Population Age 45 or Better: 41%

Cost of Living: 8% below the national average

Median Home Price: $125,000

Climate: Summer temperatures are in the 70s and 80s, and winter temperatures are in the teens, 20s and 30s. On average, the area receives 45 inches of rain and 30 inches of snow per year.

At Least One Hospital Accepts Medicare Patients? No, but Gnaden Huetten Memorial Hospital, about 10 miles away in Lehighton, accepts Medicare patients.

At Least One Hospital Accredited by Joint Commission? No, but Gnaden Huetten Memorial Hospital, about 10 miles away in Lehighton, is accredited.

Public Transit: Carbon County Community Transit offers door-to-door rides Monday through Friday. The service requires advance reservations and is limited.

Crime Rate: Well below the national average

Public Library: Yes

Political Leanings: Conservative

Is Pennsylvania Considered Tax Friendly for Retirement? Yes

Cons: Newcomers sometimes have difficulty fitting in right away. Hordes of tourists can wear thin.

Notes: Jim Thorpe is cute but very touristy.

Mechanicsburg, Pennsylvania

Sleepy Mechanicsburg is in the Cumberland Valley, an agricultural region just west of the state capital (Harrisburg) in southeastern Pennsylvania. A sturdy place, Mechanicsburg dates from 1807, and it has a good reputation.

The quaint downtown has narrow streets lined with historic brick structures and clapboard buildings that house restaurants, boutiques,

61

hardware stores, barbershops, banks, bookstores and more. Two festivals, First Friday and Jubilee Days, are held here each year. In fact, Jubilee Days is one of the longest running street fairs in eastern Pennsylvania.

The Mechanicsburg Art Center is both a school and a gallery, and the Perfect 5th Musical Arts Center holds classes and concerts. The 1863 Station Master's House and the 1801 Frankeberger Tavern, which some people say has a headless ghost, are two of the buildings preserved by the Mechanicsburg Museum Association.

Paulus Farm Market has fresh produce, bakery goods and more. Residents also enjoy some very good casual bistros and grilles.

Area attractions include golf courses and a speedway, and McCormick Park has creek access for kayakers and waders. The Mechanicsburg Trees and Trails Environmental Center has a garden, an amphitheater, hiking paths, biking trails and a bird watching blind. The Appalachian Trail passes through nearby Boiling Springs.

Neighborhoods are well-kept with Cape Cods, brick ranch ramblers, raised ranch ramblers and more.

Population: 9,000 (city proper)

Percentage of Population Age 45 or Better: 42%

Cost of Living: 3% below the national average

Median Home Price: $150,000

Climate: This area has hot, humid summers and cold winters. Summer temperatures are in the 80s and 90s, and winter temperatures are in the 20s, 30s and 40s. On average, the area receives 40 inches of rain and 26 inches of snow per year.

At Least One Hospital Accepts Medicare Patients? No, but Holy Spirit Hospital is 5 miles away in Camp Hill and accepts Medicare patients.

At Least One Hospital Accredited by Joint Commission? No, but Holy Spirit Hospital is 5 miles away in Camp Hill and is accredited.

Public Transit: The County has an on-demand van service.

Crime Rate: Meets the national average

Public Library: Yes

Political Leanings: Conservative

Is Pennsylvania Considered Tax Friendly for Retirement? Yes

Cons: The air quality is slightly below the national average.

Notes: Mechanicsburg is named after early workers who made Conestoga wagons.

South Carolina

Garden City, South Carolina

Garden City is situated along South Carolina's northeastern coast, about 8 miles south of Myrtle Beach. It is a mellow, unincorporated community known for having one of the best beaches in the state.

With creeks and tributaries all around, fishing, crabbing, birding, shelling and boating are what keep many people occupied. Fifteen golf courses are within a 10 mile drive, and Garden City is known for its Golf Cart Parade every 4th of July.

Residents enjoy some very good seafood restaurants. The Pier, which has often been voted the best pier in South Carolina, has a bar and nightly concerts during the summer. Most shopping takes place in neighboring Murrells Inlet.

Housing is a mix of suburban ranch ramblers in leafy neighborhoods, large, oceanfront single family homes and tall beachside condominiums

Population: 9,200 (city proper)

Percentage of Population Age 45 or Better: 62%

Cost of Living: 8% below the national average

Median Home Price: $130,000

Climate: This area has summer temperatures in the 80s and 90s, and winter temperatures in the 50s and 60s. On average, Garden City receives 56 inches of rain each year.

At Least One Hospital Accepts Medicare Patients? No, but Waccamaw Community Hospital, about 3 miles away in Murrells Inlet, accepts Medicare patients.

At Least One Hospital Accredited by Joint Commission? No, but Waccamaw Community Hospital, about 3 miles away in Murrells Inlet, is accredited.

Public Transit: Yes, provided by Coast RTA

Crime Rate: Below the national average

Public Library: No, but one is in Surfside Beach, about 5 miles away.

Political Leanings: Conservative

Is South Carolina Considered Tax Friendly for Retirement? Yes

Cons: The hurricane risk is real. Garden City was nearly wiped out by Hurricane Hazel in 1954 and was severely damaged by Hurricane Hugo in 1989.

Notes: This is a popular place with "snowbirds."

Goose Creek, South Carolina

Pleasant Goose Creek is only 10 miles from North Charleston, which is only 7 miles inland from Charleston on South Carolina's mid-coast. Not established as a town until 1961, Goose Creek is primarily suburban but has a U.S. Navy presence. The 17,000-acre Naval Support Activity Charleston, a couple of Navy training facilities and a Navy systems command center are located here.

This area was once home to cotton plantations, and their ruins are sometimes incorporated into new master-planned developments. Neighborhoods are tidy with housing stock that includes Cape Cods, bungalows, raised ranch ramblers, Colonials and more.

Publix, Walmart and a few other box stores are here. Restaurants are mostly national chains.

The town manages 14 parks, a pool, tennis courts and a community center. The Goose Creek Reservoir is popular with paddlers and is inhabited by bluegill and speckled perch. Snowy egrets search for food along the water's edge.

Nearby parks include the Francis Marion National Forest, the Magnolia Plantation and the Old Santee Canal State Park, which celebrates the nation's first canal system with 4 miles of boardwalks and an interpretive center. Marrington Plantation is a park with deep woods, fishing spots, abundant wildlife and well maintained biking paths and walking trails.

Population: 36,000 (city proper)

Percentage of Population Age 45 or Better: 19%

Cost of Living: 6% below the national average

Median Home Price: $130,000

Climate: Summer temperatures are in the 80s and 90s, and winter temperatures are in the 30s, 40s and 50s. On average, the area receives 50 inches of rain per year.

At Least One Hospital Accepts Medicare Patients? No, but Charleston has several hospitals that accept Medicare patients.

At Least One Hospital Accredited By Joint Commission? No, but Charleston has several hospitals that are accredited.

Public Transit: Yes, but it is limited.

Crime Rate: Below the national average

Public Library: Yes

Political Leanings: Conservative

Is South Carolina Considered Tax Friendly for Retirement? Yes

Cons: None

Notes: Goose Creek has grown by 8% in the last decade and has a lot of families with young children.

Irmo, South Carolina

In the heart of South Carolina's Midlands, Irmo is just outside of the capital city of Columbia and almost halfway between the state's mountains and its beaches. It has a small town charm and a good reputation.

Irmo is a gateway to 50,000-acre Lake Murray, a reservoir fed by the Saluda River. With more than 500 miles of shoreline, the lake is a magnet for water devotees from around the region. It has marinas, recreation areas and the Billy Dreher Island State Park. Boating, water skiing and fishing, particularly for redear sunfish and largemouth bass, are popular.

Although it is considered a suburb of Columbia, Irmo has amenities of its own. The community orchestra has a Sunday concert series, and the Okra Strut is a decades-old tradition that includes live music and a parade.

Saluda Shoals Park has kayak rentals and guided horseback rides. The miles of trails in the adjacent Harbison State Forest meander through hardwood forests and cross streams and glades. Ten golf courses are within easy reach.

Neighborhoods are nicely landscaped. Home styles include ranch rambler, plantation, Craftsman and more.

Population: 11,000 (city proper)

Percentage of Population Age 45 or Better: 27%

Cost of Living: 7% below the national average

Median Home Price: $132,000

Climate: Summer temperatures are in the 80s and 90s, and winter temperatures are in the 30s, 40s and 50s. On average, the area receives 50 inches of rain per year.

At Least One Hospital Accepts Medicare Patients? No, but Columbia has a hospital that accepts Medicare patients.

At Least One Hospital Accredited By Joint Commission? No, but Columbia has a hospital that is accredited.

Public Transit: No

Crime Rate: Meets the national average

Public Library: The northern branch of the Columbia library system
serves as the Irmo library.

Political Leanings: Liberal

Is South Carolina Considered Tax Friendly for Retirement? Yes

Cons: None

Notes: Irmo has grown by 7% in the last decade, and its population
has a median income above the national median.

Northlake, South Carolina

Northlake is a residential community situated in Upstate South
Carolina, about 30 miles southwest of Greenville. It has grown by
nearly 20% in the last decade.

This growth is mostly due to Northlake's reasonable cost of living
and waterfront location. It sits on both sides of a northern offshoot of
56,000-acre Lake Hartwell, a man-made reservoir that is one of the
most popular recreation areas in the South. Tourists and residents
alike enjoy water skiing, fishing, camping, swimming and wildlife
watching.

Northlake neighborhoods are leafy, meandering, low density and
well-tended with new Craftsmans, plantation styles and brick ranch
ramblers. Homes directly on the water tend to be larger and have
covered boat docks.

Nearly all shopping and dining options are in Anderson, population
26,000 and the County seat, about 5 miles away.

Population: 3,800 (city proper)

Percentage of Population Age 45 or Better: 43%

Cost of Living: Meets the national average

Median Home Price: $170,000

Climate: Summer temperatures are in the 80s and 90s. Winter temperatures are in 30s, 40s and 50s. On average, the area receives 50 inches of rain each year.

At Least One Hospital Accepts Medicare Patients? No, but Anmed Health in Anderson, 5 miles away, accepts Medicare patients.

At Least One Hospital Accredited by Joint Commission? No, but Anmed Health in Anderson, 5 miles away, is accredited.

Public Transit: No

Crime Rate: Below the national average

Public Library: No, but one is 5 miles away in Anderson.

Political Leanings: Very conservative

Is South Carolina Considered Tax Friendly for Retirement? Yes

Cons: The tornado risk is 70% higher than the national average.

Notes: Northlake is a nice, relatively affordable area along a lake.

Port Royal, South Carolina

Sleepy Port Royal sits along Port Royal Sound on the southern South Carolina coast and is just across the water from 8,100-acre Marine Corps Recruit Depot Parris Island (which is actually part of the city). The Spanish first came to this area in the early-16th century, and the flags of six nations, Spain, France, England, Scotland, the United States and the Confederacy, have flown over Port Royal.

With the town situated between the Beaufort River and Battery Creek, marshes and estuaries abound. Boating and fishing are a Port Royal way of life and have been since its earliest days.

The Old Village, along Paris Avenue, hosts a StreetMusic concert series and the always popular Soft Shell Crab Fest. Inviting shops and restaurants are in good supply (11th Street Dockside eatery in particular gets rave reviews).

This section of town also includes iconic, working shrimp docks, but revitalization is scheduled to make the area more appealing. A bird sanctuary for pelicans, falcons and eagles is also planned.

The Sands municipal beach has picnic areas, a boat ramp, a boardwalk and miles of nature trails. The Shed hosts concerts and plays. Thirteen golf courses are within a 10 mile drive.

Port Royal boasts of its "new urbanism" and has some appealing, high density housing with a very European feel. Bungalows, plantation styles and contemporary designs are here, too.

Population: 10,600 (city proper)

Percentage of Population Age 45 or Better: 28%

Cost of Living: 5% below the national average

Median Home Price: $120,000

Climate: Summers have temperatures in the 80s and 90s, and winters are mild with temperatures in the 40s, 50s and 60s. On average, the area receives 48 inches of rain per year.

Public Transit: The County has a van program that provides transportation to social events, medical appointments and recreational activities.

Crime Rate: Below the national average

Public Library: No, but one is 5 miles away in Beaufort.

At Least One Hospital Accepts Medicare Patients? No, but Beaufort Memorial Hospital, just a couple of miles to the north, accepts Medicare patients.

At Least One Accredited by Joint Commission? No, but Beaufort Memorial Hospital, just a couple of miles to the north, is accredited.

Political Leanings: Conservative

Is South Carolina Considered Tax Friendly for Retirement? Yes

Cons: None

Notes: The city blends into Beaufort to the north.   Parris Island trains 17,000 Marines each year. Retirees enjoy the area because it is close to Hilton Head Island.   A naval hospital is in town.

Tennessee

Loudon, Tennessee

Nestled in the foothills of eastern Tennessee's lush Great Smoky Mountains, charming Loudon was once a busy Tennessee River steamship port.   It is named after nearby Fort Loudoun, a reconstructed Colonial-era British fort.

Today Loudon is an attractive town with a small, walkable core. Residents enjoy a farmers' market, antique stores, ice cream shops, as well as historic buildings such as the Carmichael Inn and Orme Wilson Storehouse. The intimate, red brick Lyric Theatre is home to two theatrical groups and hosts anything from concerts and plays to movies.

The town's Riverside Park and the nearby Poplar Springs Recreation Area have boat ramps, docks, and fishing piers. There are seven golf courses in the County, and three of them are within Loudon's city limits.

The annual Smoky Mountain Fiddler's Convention is held in Loudon's Legion Park, and the convention coincides with an antique fair and crafts festival.

Many neighborhoods have a country feeling. Older areas have modest homes on large lots. The resort-style communities of Tennessee National and Tellico Village also have a Loudon address. Both have golf course homes and waterfront homes, many of which are large and made from brick.

Population: 5,500 (city proper)

Percentage of Population Age 45 or Better: 48%

Cost of Living: Meets the national average

Median Home Price: $199,000

Climate: Summer temperatures are in the 80s and 90s, and humidity is high. Winters are mild with temperatures in the 40s, 50s and 60s. On average, the area receives 50 inches of rain per year.

At Least One Hospital Accepts Medicare Patients? No, but Lenoir, 6 miles away, has a hospital that accepts Medicare patients.

At Least One Hospital Accredited by Joint Commission? No, but Lenoir, 6 miles away, has a hospital that is accredited.

Public Transit: No

Crime Rate: Below the national average

Public Library: Yes, located in Tellico Village

Political Leanings: Very, very conservative

Is Tennessee Considered Tax Friendly for Retirement?   Somewhat

Cons: The tornado risk is 25% higher than the national average.

Notes: Loudon has grown by 10% within the last decade.

White House, Tennessee

Originally a stagecoach stop on the Louisville and Nashville Turnpike, comfortable White House is now along Interstate 65 and 25 miles north of Nashville. It straddles two counties and is a rural, residential place, peppered with tall trees, green spaces and attractive homes.

The town has grown by 30% in the last decade, thanks in large part to Nashville families who want a pleasant, affordable place to raise children. Many homes are antebellum style, farmhouse style or brick ranch rambler style and sit on large lots.

White House manages 120 acres of park land, and its community center includes a gym, a cafeteria, an auditorium and a senior center. The heavily wooded town greenway adds to the quiet, country atmosphere.

Although the historic White House Inn was torn down in 1951, a replica was erected in 1986 and houses a small library and a museum. Tools, furniture and photographs from the town's early days crowd the second floor space.

Churches, particularly Baptist, are plentiful, and community groups include the Lions Club and the Rotary Club. Large retailers are limited, and restaurants are mostly national chains.

The active chamber of commerce sponsors an Americana Celebration, and the town hosts a Labor Day bicycle parade and a 5k foot race. Old Hickory Lake, about 20 miles away, offers plenty of opportunities for fishing, boating and waterskiing.

Population: 10,500 (city proper)

Percentage of Population Age 45 or Better: 23%

Cost of Living: 5% below the national average

Median Home Price: $155,000

Climate: Summer temperatures reach the mid-90s. Winters are mild with temperatures in the 40s, 50s and 60s. On average, the area receives 50 inches of rain per year.

At Least One Hospital Accepts Medicare Patients? No, but TriStar Hendersonville Medical Center is 14 miles away and accepts Medicare patients.

At Least One Hospital Accredited by Joint Commission? No, but TriStar Hendersonville Medical Center is 14 miles away and is accredited.

Public Transit: Mid-Cumberland Human Resources Agency operates a reservation-based, door-to-door van service.

Crime Rate: Well below the national average

Public Library: Yes

Political Leanings: Very, very conservative

Is Tennessee Considered Tax Friendly for Retirement? Somewhat

Cons: The tornado risk is 145% higher than the national average.

Notes: White House has a nice reputation. While growing, it still has a small town feeling. More services and supplies are available in Hendersonville, about 10 miles away.

Texas

Canyon, Texas

Arid, flat West Texas is home to Canyon, a metropolis that sits where a large cattle ranch once thrived. Just 18 miles from downtown Amarillo, the town grew up around the railroad and in 1910 welcomed the opening of West Texas State Normal College.

Today this higher learning institution is known as West Texas A&M University and has 9,000 students. Even with the University here, Canyon does not feel like a typical college town. Quiet and friendly, it has a country atmosphere and little nightlife.

Canyon is the gateway to Palo Duro Canyon State Park, a dramatic, rugged canyon system that is second in size only to the Grand Canyon. Painter Georgia O'Keeffe lived and taught in Canyon from 1916 to 1918 and said of Palo Duro Canyon, "It is a burning, seething cauldron, filled with dramatic light and color."

The musical drama, "TEXAS," which is performed in an outdoor amphitheater 6 nights a week during the summer, is a Canyon highlight. It chronicles the tragedies and triumphs of early Texas settlers and is said to be the most attended outdoor drama in the nation.

Residents enjoy two golf courses, exhibits at the Panhandle-Plains Historical Museum and nearly 50 restaurants, everything from fast food chains to locally owned barbeque joints. The downtown square has some cute shops.

West Texas A&M supports a writers' academy and a continuing education department with a lecture series. University athletic games are well attended.

Neighborhoods are tidy, and many have brick ranch ramblers.

Population: 13,500 (city proper)

Percentage of Population Age 45 or Better: 24%

Cost of Living: 12% below the national average

Median Home Price: $125,000

Climate: Summer temperatures are in the 80s and 90s, and winter temperatures are in the 20s, 30s and 40s. The elevation is 3,550 feet above sea level. On average, the area receives 20 inches of rain each year.

At Least One Hospital Accepts Medicare Patients? No, but Amarillo has several hospitals that accept Medicare patients.

At Least One Hospital Accredited by Joint Commission? No, but Amarillo has several hospitals that are accredited.

Public Transit: Yes

Crime Rate: Well below the national average

Public Library: Yes

Political Leanings: Very, very conservative

Is Texas Considered Tax Friendly for Retirement? Yes

Cons: The tornado risk is 155% above the national average.

Notes: Canyon has a reputation as a comfortable place. It draws summer tourists who come to hike in the canyon and to watch the "TEXAS" show.

Fredericksburg, Texas

In 1846, German immigrants fleeing oppressive political and social conditions came to the Hill Country in south central Texas and founded Fredericksburg. Located 75 miles west of Austin, the town, also known as Fritztown, sits in a pretty landscape, surrounded by peach groves, herb farms and lavender fields.

Fredericksburg is one of the most popular tourist destinations in Texas and is known for its wealth of unique 19th-century German architecture. In fact, much of the town is listed on the National Register of Historic Places.

The downtown has more than 100 antique stores, boutique shops, candy stores, galleries and the like, as well as some very good German restaurants. The community theater, farmers' market, wineries and military museums all have fans. The Roxbox Theater's cast presents old fashioned rock and roll shows and receives rave reviews.

Homes styles are eclectic, ranging from very interesting contemporary bungalows to 19th-century stone dwellings.

Population: 10,500 (city proper)

Percentage of Population Age 45 or Better: 52%

Cost of Living: Meets the national average

Median Home Price: $185,000

Climate: The climate is humid subtropical. Summer temperatures are in the 80s, 90s and even low-100s. Winter temperatures are in the 30s, 40s and 50s. On average, the area receives 30 inches of rain per year.

At Least One Hospital Accepts Medicare Patients? Yes

At Least One Hospital Accredited by Joint Commission? Yes

Public Transit: No

Crime Rate: Well below the national average

Public Library: Yes

Political Leanings: Very, very conservative

Is Texas Considered Tax Friendly for Retirement? Yes

Cons: Locals say that Fredericksburg is not particularly dog-friendly. Tourists come in droves during the summer.

Notes: Big city amenities are in Austin, which is easily reached via U.S. Route 290. Fredericksburg is growing, blossoming by 18% in the last decade. Texas German is a local dialect that stems from the early days and is still spoken by some residents.

Springtown, Texas

On the quiet, rolling prairie of north central Texas, about 30 miles outside of Fort Worth, friendly, easygoing Springtown makes its home. It was established in the 1850s and named for the cold water springs that bubbled from nearby hillsides.

Springtown grew up as a farming and ranching community, and even though it has become a fast-growing commuter town for Fort Worth, it retains its rural character. The simple town core is a little haphazard but has town offices, a pizza restaurant, a karate place, a donut shop, a furniture store and the like.

Established neighborhoods have few sidewalks, small lots and modest ranch ramblers, while newer subdivisions on the outskirts of town have larger brick homes on more expansive lots. Some residences come with acreage.

The annual Wild West Festival celebrates Springtown's roots with a parade and a barbeque cook-off. The Legends Museum, housed in a 1910 home, showcases local history and sponsors the annual Tour of Homes.

Restaurants include fast food places, diners, cafes and Woody Creek Bar-B-Q, which receives rave reviews. Gas stations, banks, Brookshire's Food and Pharmacy and the like ensure that basic needs are covered.

Porcupine Stadium hosts high school football games, soccer games and track events. The non-profit community center has a swimming pool, a gym, a weight room and group classes.

To the east of Springtown, Eagle Mountain Lake is the place for boating and fishing. To the north, the Caddo-LBJ National Grasslands has areas for hiking, camping and horseback riding.

Population: 2,700 (city proper)

Percentage of Population Age 45 or Better: 32%

Cost of Living: 13% below the national average

Median Home Price: $105,000

Climate: Summer temperatures are in the 90s and low-100s, and winter temperatures are in the 30s, 40s and 50s. On average, the area receives 33 inches of rain and a dusting of snow each year. Ice storms happen occasionally.

At Least One Hospital Accepts Medicare Patients? No, but Texas Health Harris Methodist Azle is 10 miles away and accepts Medicare patients.

At Least One Hospital Accredited by Joint Commission? No, but Texas Health Harris Methodist Azle is 10 miles away and is accredited.

Public Transit: No

Crime Rate: Meets the national average

Public Library: Yes

Political Leanings: Very, very conservative

Is Texas Considered Tax Friendly for Retirement? Yes

Cons: The tornado risk is 240% higher than the national average.

Notes: Springtown sits along State Highway 199, which provides easy access to Fort Worth. The town has grown by 28% within the last decade.

Virginia

Floyd, Virginia

In the rolling Appalachian hills of rural western Virginia, the tiny, closely-knit town of Floyd is the Floyd County seat.   It is a cute, artsy place with a lot of creative energy and has grown by 15% within the 10 years.

Home to musicians, artisans, old hippies and deeply ingrained families, Floyd is particularly known for its bluegrass and "old tyme" music.   Fiddle players and string quartets often play music on the sidewalks or in the parks.   Weekends are particularly festive when everyone seems to be out and about playing music or dancing to it.

The Friday Night Jamboree and Radio Show, hosted at the Floyd Country Store, has a regional reputation. The Sun Music Hall and the Oddfellas Cantina sponsor open microphone nights, and FloydFest attracts musicians from around the country.

The downtown is small but lined with colorfully painted wood structures and brick buildings that house galleries, musical instrument stores, wine tasting rooms and cafes.

There are enough stores and service providers to meet basic needs. Two farmers' markets ensure that dairy products, fresh produce, organic meats and jellies are available.

The Jacksonville Center for the Arts has classes, concerts and juried art shows. The region boasts 3 wineries and a cider house.

Floyd's recreation department has Senior Olympics and aerobics classes. A hike up the nearby Buffalo Mountain offers views of the County, and the Little River is popular for canoeing, kayaking, and fishing. The Blue Ridge Parkway is perfect for a Sunday afternoon drive.

Housing includes raised ranch ramblers, Federal styles, cabins and brick bungalows. Most homes sit on large lots.

Population: 450 (city proper)

Percentage of Population Age 45 or Better: 54%

Cost of Living: 10% below the national average

Median Home Price: $128,000

Climate: Summer temperatures are in the 70s and 80s, and winter temperatures are in the 20s and 30s. On average, the area receives 40 inches of rain and 18 inches of snow each year.

At Least One Hospital Accepts Medicare Patients? No, but Carilion New River Valley Medical Center is 16 miles away in Christiansburg and accepts Medicare patients.

At Least One Hospital Accredited by Joint Commission? No, but Carilion New River Valley Medical Center is 16 miles away in Christiansburg and is accredited.

Public Transit: No

Crime Rate: Below the national average

Public Library: Yes

Political Leanings: Conservative

Is Virginia Considered Tax Friendly for Retirement? Somewhat

Cons: None

Notes: Many counter culture types came to Floyd in the 1960s and never left. This area also has a reputation as the "moonshine capital" of Virginia.

Hillsville, Virginia

Hillsville is in lush, rural southwestern Virginia, less than 20 minutes from the North Carolina border and about 90 minutes from Roanoke. It has long been supported by agriculture and is the Carroll County seat.

Surrounded by the Blue Ridge Mountains, Hillsville is best known for its bi-annual flea market, which is officially known as the VFW Flea Market and Gun Show. The market consumes the entire community and usually draws crowds numbering in the hundreds of thousands.

The downtown is lined with two story and three story red brick buildings and feels somewhat stuck in time. Town history is honored with a museum, a Confederate monument and Virginia's oldest continuously operated streetcar diner.

The farmers' market is open year-round, and the Red Hill General Store has everything from canning supplies and grass fed beef to garden clogs. Most retailers are locally owned.

Considering its size, Hillsville has a lot of festivals and events, including an arts and crafts show, the Bluegrass and Old Time Fiddlers' Competition, the Beach Music Festival and more.

Nearby Rocky Knob Recreation Area has extensive camping areas and easy access to Chateau Morrisette Winery and Mabry Mill, an often-photographed water power mill. The George Washington and

Jefferson National Forests, both close at hand, have some of the best trout streams in the state.

Neighborhoods are low density, and most of them do not have sidewalks. Home styles include ranch rambler, raised ranch rambler, cottage, bungalow, plantation and more.

Population: 2,700 (city proper)

Percentage of Population Age 45 or Better: 57%

Cost of Living: 10% below the national average

Median Home Price: $125,000

Climate: Summer temperatures are in the 70s and 80s, and winter temperatures are in the 20s and 30s. On average, the area receives 43 inches of rain and 18 inches of snow each year.

At Least One Hospital Accepts Medicare Patients? No, but Twin County Regional Hospital is 12 miles away and accepts Medicare patients.

At Least One Hospital Accredited by Joint Commission? No, but Twin County Regional Hospital is 12 miles away and is accredited.

Public Transit: The County has a limited van service to shopping areas and medical facilities.

Crime Rate: Meets the national average

Public Library: Yes

Political Leanings: Very conservative

Is Virginia Considered Tax Friendly for Retirement? Somewhat

Cons: The poverty rate is slightly above the national average.

Notes: The air quality is very good.

Website Bibliography

areavibes.com

bestplaces.net

census.gov

city-data.com

crimereports.com

economist.com

epa.gov

fbi.gov

google.com maps

Individual city and chamber of commerce websites, library websites, hospital websites, transportation websites

jointcommission.org

kiplingers.com

nationalregisterofhistoricplaces.com

nps.gov

realtor.com

taxfoundation.org

trulia.com

weather.com

wikipedia.com

zillow.com

About the Author

Kris Kelley lives in beautiful Colorado has been finding and reviewing great places to retire since 2006. She is an avid traveler, always looking for that hidden gem of a town, whether it be along an ocean, in a desert or on a mountaintop.

CPSIA information can be obtained
at www.ICGtesting.com
Printed in the USA
BVOW06s0728090717
488883BV00017B/983/P